LOST MEMORIES

Miranda Maynard

This edition first published in paperback by
Michael Terence Publishing in 2023
www.mtp.agency

Copyright © 2023 Miranda Maynard

Miranda Maynard has asserted the right to be identified as
the author of this work in accordance with the
Copyright, Designs and Patents Act 1988

ISBN 9781800945050

No part of this publication may be reproduced, stored
in a retrieval system, or transmitted, in any form or
by any means, electronic, mechanical, photocopying,
recording or otherwise, without the prior
permission of the publisher

Cover image
Copyright © DB Virago
www.123rf.com

Cover design
Copyright © 2023 Michael Terence Publishing

Contents

Part 1 : 1

EARLY SECONDARY SCHOOL YEARS 1

    Third Year..3

    Of Timothy's Lost Interest
    (and Passion) for Football 6

    Weeks of Bullying.. 11

    Timothy Drops Out of Science Club........................... 13

    School Chess Club 15

    Timothy Alone by Himself.. 16

Part 2 : 19

FOURTH YEAR.. 19

    Christmas Production..28

    Summer Fete 29

Also by Miranda Maynard.. 31

Part 1:

EARLY SECONDARY SCHOOL YEARS

Third Year

Timothy attended his English lesson. The school teacher gave out exercise books to the whole class.

Sitting next to Tim, a member of his Form obtained an 'A' Grade for his English homework. Tim looked at his grade marked in red. Tim obtained a 'C+'. Timothy felt disappointed by his grade obtained. Timothy envied how he kept obtaining 'A' Grades in English all the time. Timothy lacked self-esteem. He also lacked self-confidence.

Timothy thought of himself as a dunce. Generally, this English class was of mixed ability. This English Teacher was also a P.E. Teacher for Girls. (The following year, his remedial Teacher was also an English Teacher.)

Accordingly, all of the pupils streamed in groups and sets.

Timothy got frustrated, embarrassed and humiliated at his lack of progress. (Tim's school Report was bad.)

The bright pupils were humiliators.

Usually, Tim preferred English to any other subject. English (Language) remained Timothy's favourite subject. Timothy did badly at this subject. (A C.S.E. candidate.)

After that period, Timothy went to the Geography Department. The pupil was the last one to enter the

Geography classroom. Timothy sat down at the table somewhere in the middle of the classroom. The bright sunshine shone through the large paned windows.

The pupil, a schoolgirl was sitting at the table in front. Her long blonde hair brilliant in the radiant sunshine. Her fairness a golden resplendence.

Timothy in a daydreaming, dreamy state glanced at the Blonde. He drooled at the schoolgirl. Admiring her golden blondeness.

During the lesson, the class read through the Geography textbook. Timothy disliked this subject. He thought this subject hard and uninterestingly uninspiring. Perhaps complicated, boring with technical terminologies.

Timothy took the time to daydream. With his hand resting on his chin. The daydreamer looked out of the window. At present, the Geography class got on with their classwork.

At break time, Timothy sat outside on the Science Block. He stayed seated on the wooden bench and ate an apple. Standing there were other younger pupils in their groups of various ages in their school year, they stayed outside the Science Block and talked amongst themselves.

Timothy attended his next period. He did Physics. Learning about the Plumb line. He was uninterested in this science subject. As usual, he felt unenthusiastic about it. The classroom was gloomy with a dull, murky light.

Timothy attended his next period. He did Maths and mental arithmetic. He obtained an average score. He befriended a classmate whom he sat next to in Maths class. The pupil was simple-minded, worldly, decadent and a constellation.

(At lunchtime, Timothy usually played Football with Nick and his school fellows in the school playground. Some of these schoolboys were a constellation with an enthusiasm for playing football.)

Of Timothy's Lost Interest (and Passion) for Football

When it was time for games, all the schoolboys entered the pavilion and changed into their school P.E. kit; a reversible top, matching shorts and thick socks. Timothy remained the last one to get changed and came out of the pavilion alone. The P.E. Teacher made the large group of schoolboys do a cross-country run. All of the schoolboys were exhausted afterwards. The best runners were either sprinters or cross-country runners. There was no potential marathon runner among the groups running.

At this time of the morning, Timothy struggled to run. He felt such fatigue. The other schoolboys ran better than him. The large group of runners ran a long distance with the fit P.E. teacher accompanying them.

After the cross-country ended the schoolboys played football on a playing field, a muddy and patchy football pitch. All of the schoolboys were far too exhausted. This game of football was scrappy. It was a typical schoolboys' game of football. Both teams were playing in style.

Timothy wore new football boots. He played football badly. The schoolboys played football and their football boots floundered in the wet mud. This typical game of football was a possession play. Timothy ended up on the losing team. The team that lost were disappointed as they all trudged off the muddy ground, a patchy football pitch.

None of the better players was selected for the school football team. Those schoolboys rejected for the first school team were disappointed and demoralised.

Timothy lost interest in playing football. He gave it up. The fan even lost his enthusiasm for supporting his favourite football team. He even gave that up. He lost his passion and interest in the sport.

Attending his periods, Timothy could not concentrate on any of his subjects as he felt too fatigued as well as exhausted. Timothy rested during his lessons. The pupil did not do any classwork as he was idle and lazy. He spent his time recovering from exhaustion and fatigue. Finally, when the bell sounded, Timothy felt relieved that it was the end of the final lesson. Leaving school at once, the schoolboy made his way to the nearest bus stop alone. At that time Timothy got the early bus home.

After the school bell sounded, Timothy attended Design, Home Economics. The actual cooking preparation had been done in advance to save time. These pupils in the Home Economic Group were prepared to bake their sponge cakes in gas ovens. The helpful pupils assisted one another with their Teacher assisting them with obligational assistance to every pupil.

Timothy was pleased with himself as he put a sponge cake in a tin. Then he put it in his locker outside his Form room.

At lunchtime, Timothy left the secondary school to go down to the school playground. Over there, he played Football in a playground with a group of schoolboys.

Timothy enjoyed playing Football with them. Usually, Timothy was lonely and a loner. Every day he played Football with his school fellows and his friends. Today at lunchtime, it was a good game of Football. Every lunchtime Timothy played Football regularly with the same group of schoolboys.

Timothy was appreciative of Nick who allowed him to play Football with his schoolfellows. Some of the schoolboys' blazers were hanging up on the aluminium wire fence.

After lunchtime had finally ended, all of the schoolchildren headed back to school. Going back to their Form Rooms where they attended Registration. Timothy sitting in his Form Room had a rest. He took a bottle of lemon squash out of his sports bag. He drank chilled icy lemon squash in a big, plastic bottle.

After Registration, the Form then attended their next period. Timothy attended Remedial. (Extra English classes instead of Foreign Languages.)

That afternoon at the Extra Teaching class, the group worked from a worksheet which they each answered, following questions from the next. Every worksheet had various themes. The Teacher marked it. Timothy got high marks. Although Timothy became embarrassed, frustrated and humiliated at doing remedial, he did enjoy it. He relaxed. In the classroom, it was a peaceful relaxation. During the next period, Timothy attended Art in his Form Room. Already laid there on tables were white sheets of paper of painted pictures.

Timothy tried to paint a still life in his Art lesson. He just could not paint. He disliked the subject. Sitting next to him a member of his Form painted. He was good at Art. The Art class did still life.

In the last period, Timothy attended his Music lesson. The class was marked for playing either a recorder or a harmonica.

When it was Timothy's turn, he got very nervous at trying to play the recorder. He felt embarrassed and humiliated.

Everybody else did better than he did at attempting to play the recorder. Timothy was relieved when the Music lesson ended.

Going home from school, he felt frustrated, humiliated and embarrassed. This humiliating experience remained Timothy's worst school day.

At home, Timothy was all alone. From subsequent circumstances, things had evidently changed. He had been neglected by his Mother who was always neglectful towards her son. Timothy came from a single-parent family. He disliked his life, school and of course his schooldays. A particularly embarrassing, humiliating and frustrating experience.

Timothy had an unhappy home life. His Father had abandoned him since he was a Teenager. His delinquent

Brother deserted him and his older brother beat him up.

The next day at school, Timothy was bullied by certain members of his Form. Did the Form Tutor witness it?

The Bullies taunted and teased him. Timothy felt scared. He avoided them. He isolated himself. Timothy was a loner. He felt so lonely. As a schoolboy, he felt deeply unhappy and miserable. As a third-year pupil, he experienced bullying. These were terribly unhappy schooldays. He played truant at that time.

Weeks of Bullying

The bullying had only lasted a few weeks. Timothy experienced bullying. In the form room, members of his form bullied him. His form mate at that time wasn't there to defend and protect him. Certain members of his form taunted and teased him. They bullied him. Timothy was afraid, nervous and timid, a trembling, scared schoolboy. He avoided his form, keeping away from them. He took some measures to isolate himself. Taking precautions, he avoided everybody, especially his form on purpose.

One afternoon at school, Timothy found himself getting intimidated in the playground by a few members of his form bullying him. They surrounded him. Timothy remained unharmed. Of the bullies intimidating him, he felt scared. Timothy remained pent up with anger. He wanted to retaliate. Somehow the pupil got away from them. Wanting to retaliate. Seeking revenge.

During periods, his form mate usually sat next to him at lesson time, but from then on his form mate rejected and deserted him. Consequently, Timothy's schooldays were a misery because of bullying. However, the bullying ceased in the fourth year. As a fourth-year pupil, his time in that school year remained a happy one. A much happier pupil.

In a beautiful classroom, attending this lesson the pupil cooled off. Timothy was fond of a schoolgirl with a Mediterranean suntanned sultriness. This pupil was pacified at being in the presence of a pleasant schoolteacher and a small group of pupils who seemed nice and well-behaved. Timothy had done remedial. He rounded off the long afternoon at secondary school. A dreamy pupil daydreaming. It ended up being a good lesson.

Leaving school to get to the nearest bus stop on a quiet road, the pupil waited with a crowd of schoolchildren patiently waiting for their bus. Timothy waited with them for a bus. Although the pupil got a sense of pride at being together with all of them, he actually felt like a humiliated pupil. When the bus came, all the schoolchildren got on board to go home.

Timothy Drops Out of Science Club

With a pupil's eager desire for enrolment, Timothy had a sense of motivation to join and belong to the Science Club. Timothy enrolled in the Science Club. The Pupil found it too hard, difficult, uninteresting and boring. He soon got bored and tired of attending the Science Club. Timothy was bad at Science, as he was innumerate in this subject.

Due to having an eventual change of teacher for Biology, through unfortunate circumstances, Timothy may have become apathetic and uninterested in the Science Club. Timothy dropped out of the Science Club which was held once a week in a science room at lunchtime. Eventually, the Science Teacher was a replacement. Mr Levin became the new Biology Schoolteacher. He was unpopular and unpreferred compared to the previous Schoolmarm.

Sometime during the course of the fourth year, the schoolchildren did their mocks, followed by work experience placement with an employer for about a fortnight. Here things changed at Secondary School. All sorts of different things were happening, including circumstantial differences. The Fifth Years ended up being school leavers and also the Fourth Years engaged in work experience, working for an Employer.

At the start of the new term, Timothy sat his Mocks.

He failed them. Towards the end of the school year, he did two weeks' work experience, a work placement for an Employer.

School Chess Club

Timothy joined a chess club. He belonged to a chess club. There the pupil met chess enthusiasts and a few good chess players. Timothy played with other chess players. Timothy remained promising at chess. He was rather good at chess. Timothy played chess games and either won or lost but seldom drew. Timothy had a passion for chess. He developed an interest in it when he was a child.

One particular schoolgirl was promising. Anne played well. Anne was a budding chess champion. She constantly defeated every chess player at chess. All the other chess players admired her, knowing full well they would be beaten by her. Certain individuals, chess players, could not surpass her in any way whatsoever at interscholastic tournaments. Whatever the circumstances, Anne remained triumphant and unbeaten. With stalemates, perpetual checks and resigns, Timothy grovelled whenever he met her at the exclusive chess club. Other times, Anne eluded him. An evasive chess player showing promise. Timothy always looked forward to meeting Anne again and again. He liked her. He marvelled at the very good chess player.

Timothy Alone by Himself

Timothy was alone by himself in his form room deeply reflecting. He wondered why a few members of the form had left this secondary school. Was the reason because their parents disapproved, objected to and remained dissatisfied with this secondary school? Their parents' dissatisfaction was a resentment. Timothy stood by the window and deeply pondered on it. Thinking why the three members of his form were subsequently transferred to other state and secondary schools in accordance with their parent's approval and deep wishes.

This pupil remained pensive and wistful. Timothy desperately missed them. He still did not know the few members of his form. Apparently, they were strangers to him. Their time at this catholic secondary school was less than two years duration.

Due to subsequent circumstances, things had evidently changed. New members of his form had joined some year in the past, subsequently two females and a male. Timothy had sort of known them. Over the course of the years, as a form member, he had not known them that well. Of course, he felt sad about the ones who had left due to a transfer to another state or comprehensive school. He only saw one of them again. The other two females he never saw ever again!

He gladdened, solaced and cheered up at the few who joined his form. The mystified form approved of the three of them. The new ones.

Part 2:

FOURTH YEAR

The school timetable had changed. The periods now for this school year were from eight periods down to six periods. This Form. Every member of the Form had to fill out a form to choose their options.

Timothy attended his biology lesson. He found this subject quite hard. Those in his group were mostly Female pupils. The school teacher taught Biology. The Anatomy.

Timothy losing interest in it had a daydream. By looking out of the window from a sideward angle, then moving position, Timothy paid attention to the school teacher, teaching. The Feminine schoolmarm professional. Timothy liked the Biology Teacher. He greatly adored her. The school teacher was fond of the pupil. Timothy was humiliated at being bad at this subject. He became humiliated, embarrassed and frustrated at the prospect of doing C.S.E. Biology. The syllabus.

Suddenly the school bell rang. Now it was break time. Leaving the classroom, Timothy headed out of an entrance to a block. There, pupils came streaming in the long corridor and went down from the Maths Department. From there, Timothy walked through the school grounds to make his way down the long path. He went to the school playground which was crowded with schoolchildren. There, somewhere in the playground, Timothy played Football with the schoolboys. At this time, Timothy was enervated and tired. He played badly today. The other schoolboys played badly too. (None of them was picked for the school team.)

Those that played today in the morning were a few ethnic minorities and a constellation too.

"We are a bunch of thicks!" thought Timothy.

After break time had ended, all of the pupils there headed back to school to attend their next period.

Timothy attended Religious Studies. In that period, they read from the gospel of St Luke. Timothy did badly in this subject. He obtained low marks on his Tests and his homework. Religious Studies were compulsory. Timothy found this subject to be quite interesting. It was deeply spiritual. He was fascinated by the Christian (Faith) Religion.

Going to his next period, there along the school grounds and corridors, he walked past lovely dressed schoolgirls. At this time their school uniform was one of the world's most beautiful!

Timothy desired the sexier and prettier ones. Once again Timothy felt disappointed and rejected with regard to them. They all undesired him. Timothy remained unappealingly undesirable according to them.

Timothy attended Technical Drawing. He felt humiliated and embarrassed at being in the C.S.E. group set. He envied how a member of his Form was in the top set for Graphical Communication. How he excelled at this subject. Using a compass, Timothy drew on a sheet of paper. Nick had almost finished drawing.

At lunchtime, Timothy went down to the school playground to play Football with Nick and his friends. Today was a fine day. They all played a good game of

Football. There also playing Football was a galaxy and a constellation.

Timothy took notice of a lovely schoolgirl standing towards the back of the playground. The wise pupil walked about. This Blonde schoolgirl possessed an aura. A galaxy!

The Head Teacher on playground duty rang the bell.

All of the pupils walked together when heading back to school. Attending their Registration.

After Registration, Timothy attended his next period. He attended Extra Teaching classes in English. During the lesson, they read a play. Everyone in that group took turns reading their part. Timothy enjoyed the lesson. He liked it. Despite being embarrassed and humiliated. (The other pupils did Foreign Languages. French and German.)

Finally, Timothy attended his last period. Again, he felt humiliated. The humiliator was a member of his Form. This intelligent pupil excelled in Chemistry. Timothy sat at the front of the Lab. Feeling tired, Timothy dozed off during the Chemistry lesson. Leaving school, Timothy headed to get the early Bus. A short journey home.

During the first period in the morning, Timothy attended his History lesson down in the History Block at the other end of the Department.

The History Teacher gave dictation to the History class, on the Second World War.

Timothy became humiliated at doing C.S.E. History. In the next period, Timothy attended his Maths lesson. The bottom set did fractions.

During break time, Timothy had been out in the school grounds. Timothy found out that certain bright pupils had been entered for G.C.E. English Language and Maths. Timothy became humiliated. He envied them. Timothy suffered from humiliation and felt unhappy and miserable. With suicidal moods!

In the third period, Timothy did Technical Drawing. He was bad at the subject. In the fourth period, Timothy attended his Chemistry lesson. During class, the pupils did a scientific experiment in the Chemistry lesson.

The experienced Chemistry Teacher drew a diagram on a blackboard with a write-up of the Chemistry experiment.

Timothy, becoming bored with the subject, dozed off. He sat on a wooden stool at the front of the Laboratory. At lunchtime, Timothy went to the playground to play with Nick and his schoolfellows. Timothy played Football only for a short time. None of the better players was selected for the school football team.

After Registration attendance, Timothy and his Form, some schoolboys, got on board the coach parked outside in the road opposite the playground.

The coach drove to the High Street. The coach stopped outside a precinct. All of the schoolboys got off. Going to the precinct they walked towards the sports centre. At the sports centre, the schoolboys changed into their P.E. kit. The schoolboys did P.E. in the sports centre. Timothy played badminton with Chris a member of his Form on a badminton court.

After playing badminton, Timothy and Chris got dressed with the others in a changing room. Afterwards, the hurried schoolboys boarded the coach which drove them back to their secondary school in the heart of the rural region.

On Wednesday, after the Form morning Registration attendance, the Form attended their very first period. Timothy, a teenage schoolboy, attended his biology lesson. In that particular lesson, the class learned about Sexual Reproduction which coincided with Sex Education.

The whole class learned about the Human biological function of both the Male and Female sex. In Human Reproduction (system).

Mrs Lindel grew fond of Timothy whom the schoolmarm adored. (Over the course of the school year.) Timothy loved, adored and admired the schoolteacher.

As soon as the school bell sounded for the end of this period, the pupils put their things away in their school bags. Timothy attended his next period, a Remedial. During the course of the lesson, the group read a book. They each took it in turns to read out loud. The dialogue was vulgar, Americanized. Timothy enjoyed the lesson. He was laid back, restful, cheerful and relaxed. The ambience was a pleasure.

One of the pupils was Irish and another too, a pretty one, a plebian and a delinquent and a luscious schoolgirl, and a Dwarf with Down's Syndrome. In a beautiful classroom, attending the lesson the pupil cooled off.

Much later, Timothy left school earlier since he had a note explaining his absenteeism. Timothy attended his Doctor's appointment at the surgery. It was in the catchment area.

On Thursday morning, the Form attended Assembly in the Hall. The Headmaster addressed the school. The Headmaster spoke about how proud he was of the school. The educational success, academic attainment and achievements. Including vocational, Sports Days, interscholastic, Education, academies and institutions which they had an association with and certain charities and organizations.

All of the seated pupils looked on with pride, joy and satisfaction or dissatisfaction, envy and jealousy. Also, certain individuals were so proud, arrogant and triumphant from their academic achievements and accomplishments. Others too were unhappy and miserable, dissatisfied and discontented.

Leaving the Assembly, all of the pupils attended their period.

Timothy went to a block which was used for Design. In one of the upstairs classrooms, the Religious Studies lesson was held.

A brawny schoolboy sat next to him. The rough

schoolboy manhandled Timothy. Timothy felt uncomfortable, afraid and intimidated. Due to fear and intimidation, Timothy could not concentrate on the lesson. He did not pay attention to the schoolteacher who engaged in a class discussion. Timothy liked this subject. It was a spiritual subject, a religious one. Again, doing this subject made him become persecuted. It was a sense of persecution. (Timothy was in the C.S.E. set for Religious Studies.)

At break time, Timothy rested alone outside the Science block. Sitting on the bench there he recuperated and recovered. He preferred to be alone in the presence of younger schoolchildren, standing and talking together in groups.

When the school bell rang, a Prefect unlocked and opened the entrance door. Timothy rushed in with the other school children entering the entrance.

Timothy attended his next lesson. A Maths period. A stand-in Maths Teacher took the lesson instead of a Head of Maths Teacher. During the lesson, the bottom set did arithmetic. (Months later a top set Maths group used the same Maths classroom as the bottom set to do 'A' level maths.)

Timothy struggled with Maths as he was innumerate. His innumeracy was an inadequacy.

After the Maths lesson had ended, Timothy went to the Science Block. The Chemistry class stood by the concrete wall waiting outside the Chemistry room for the Chemistry Teacher to unlock the Lab door.

During the lesson, Timothy lost interest in the subject. The subject was far too hard. As a C.S.E. candidate, he saw himself as a dunce. Sitting on a stool, Timothy lounged about throughout the whole Chemistry lesson.

At lunchtime, Timothy left the school to go down to the playground. There he met to his surprise Mrs Laurel doing playground duty. The schoolmarm put her arms around Timothy in the presence of his members of Form. Timothy felt deeply loved and protected. Last year in the Third Year he had been bullied by bullies of his Form.

That afternoon, Timothy did not play Football with the group of schoolboys playing Football in the playground. Alone, he isolated himself somewhere in the school grounds. Timothy was elated and euphoric.

In the Form Room at Registration, Timothy felt much happier. He felt loved!

He had never felt so happy ever before. Timothy was so beatific as he attended his last two periods at school.

On Friday, it was the end of term. The school attended Mass in a Chapel. The Catholic pupils worshipped. They were prayerful and worshipful.

After the Mass ended, every pupil genuflected in accordance with their reverence before leaving their aisle. The school broke up at 3 pm for the end of term.

Christmas Production

In the Autumn, certain pupils at drama classes were chosen for certain parts in a Pantomime. Timothy, a theatrical pupil had been rejected for a role which he had auditioned for. He now remained apathetic about the pantomime itself. He could not care less about it now. Feeling anger, the pupil remained apathetic about the seasonal Christmas production.

The pupils doing drama rehearsed over the course of the weeks. Also, they engaged in dress rehearsals. Those who successfully got parts in the pantomime were rather good. The odd one showed talent and promise, a promising budding actor, a leading role. The supporting budding actress was also good. A comical and funny Fairy Godmother.

The pantomime was held in a grand hall at Christmastime. As Timothy remained labelled for theatricals. Timothy lacked interest and at present was indifferent to its bill.

On midweek that Christmas Wednesday, it was a full house at the School Hall. The performance itself was a good one. After their performance, the pupils acting, budding actors and actresses, received a standing ovation. With triumph, they were a motivational inspiration!

On stage, the cast took a bow in front of the seated and standing audience. All proceeds went to a charity, to a charitable organisation.

Summer Fete

One July summer's day, a summer Fete was held in the grounds of an imposing institute. (The same residence where King Henry Eighth once stayed.) All of the proceeds went to Charity.

There were crowds of people everywhere. Suddenly Timothy met Mrs Laurel, his school teacher somewhere down in the beautiful gardens. Mrs Laurel smoked a cigarette.

"Stand away!" said Mrs Laurel politely.

In reverence, Timothy obeyed Mrs Laurel and stood away. Mrs Laurel threw a wellington boot as far as she could. Mrs Laurel struggled to throw it!

From that day on, Timothy never saw Mrs Laurel ever again!

Timothy loved Mrs Laurel. He still has fond memories of his beloved schoolteacher.

- THE END -

Also by Miranda Maynard

*Available worldwide from
Amazon and all good bookstores*

www.mtp.agency

www.facebook.com/mtp.agency

@mtp_agency

www.ingramcontent.com/pod-product-compliance
Lightning Source LLC
LaVergne TN
LVHW051218070526
838200LV00063B/4951